TRENDS IN FOOD TECHNOLOGY

Safe Food

Hazel King

Heinemann
LIBRARY

www.heinemann.co.uk/library
Visit our website to find out more information about Heinemann Library books.

To order:
☎ Phone 44 (0) 1865 888066
🖹 Send a fax to 44 (0) 1865 314091
🖥 Visit the Heinemann Bookshop at www.heinemann.co.uk/library to browse our catalogue and order online.

Heinemann Library is an imprint of Pearson Education Limited, a company incorporated in England and Wales having its registered office at Edinburgh Gate, Harlow, Essex, CM20 2JE – Registered company number: 00872828

"Heinemann" is a registered trademark of Pearson Education Limited

Edited by Andrew Farrow and Claire Throp
Designed by Richard Parker and Q2A
Illustrated by David Woodroffe
Picture research by Hannah Taylor
Production by Alison Parsons
Originated by Heinemann Library
Printed in China by CTPS

ISBN 978 0 431 14061 2 (hardback)
12 11 10 09 08
10 9 8 7 6 5 4 3 2 1

ISBN 978 0 431 14067 4 (paperback)
12 11 10 09 08
10 9 8 7 6 5 4 3 2 1

British Library Cataloguing in Publication Data
King, Hazel
Safe food. – 2nd ed. – (Trends in food technology)
363.1'92
A full catalogue record for this book is available from the British Library.

Acknowledgements
We would like to thank the following for permission to reproduce photographs:
© Britstock-ifa p. **36**; © Corbis/Robert Pickett p. **10**; © Getty Images/Dorling Kindersley p. **38**; © Pearson Education Ltd/Gareth Boden pp. **9, 27**; © Pearson Education Ltd/Tudor Photography pp. **13, 15, 25**; © Pearson Education Ltd/Trevor Clifford p. **7**; © Photolibrary/Anthony Blake p. **33**; © Photolibrary/Anthony Blake/Maximilian Stock p. **20**; © Photolibrary/Anthony Blake/PFT Associates p. **29**; © Photolibrary/Anthony Blake/Tony Robbins p. **30**; © Photolibrary/Cephas Picture Library p. **11**; © Photolibrary/Polka Dot Images p. **38**; © Rex Features/Image Source p. **43**; © Science Photo Library/Agstockusa/Debra Ferguson p. **32**; © Science Photo Library/David Scharf p. **21**; © Science Photo Library/Gustoimages p. **19**; © Sheffield City Council p. **41**; © Somerset Creameries p. **17**.

Cover photograph of a researcher holding stalks of wheat reproduced with permission of © Getty Images/ Taxi/ Victor Paris.

We would like to thank Alison Winson, and Frank R. Conn of Cox Technologies, USA, for their invaluable help in the preparation of the first edition of this book.

Contents

Any words appearing in the text in bold, **like this**, are explained in the glossary.

Friendly bacteria

Introducing safety

The issue of food safety has been a major concern since the 1980s, with a long list of serious problems occurring, including salmonella and eggs, **BSE** and beef, *E.coli 0157*, and listeria. Food safety has become a matter of great importance to consumers and it is essential that awareness is raised to allay fears as well as to improve knowledge. Many people worry about **bacteria** and its effect on food but not all bacteria is harmful. 'Friendly' bacteria actually help in the production of useful food products such as cheese, yoghurt and **novel proteins** (see page 8).

Micro-what?

Micro-organisms are very small, living organisms of either plant or animal origin. Many are only visible through a microscope. Some micro-organisms are beneficial to the food industry because they are used in the production of certain foods. Other micro-organisms can cause food poisoning if they are present in large enough numbers. A third group of micro-organisms cause food spoilage, commonly seen when food 'goes off'.

Biological groups

There are five main types of micro-organism as listed below.

Algae

Algae are plants, some of which can be seen with the naked eye, such as seaweed. Many algae live in water and grow as a mass, such as the green slime often seen near the surface of ponds. Certain types of algae are harvested and used as a source of protein.

Protozoa

Protozoa are single-celled plants. They live mainly in water such as ponds, rivers, the sea and in soil. An amoeba is an example of a protozoa. Most do not cause disease but some are **pathogenic** and cause diseases such as amoebic dysentery.

Viruses

Viruses are the micro-organisms that cause viral diseases such as measles, chicken pox and hepatitis A. They are the smallest of all micro-organisms and can only survive as **parasites** on other living beings.

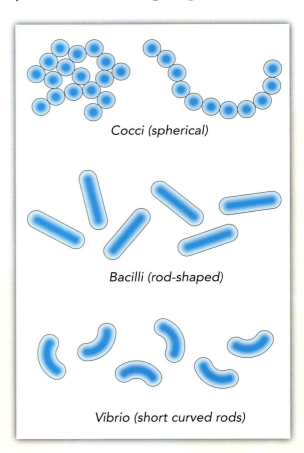

Cocci (spherical)

Bacilli (rod-shaped)

Vibrio (short curved rods)

 Bacteria are grouped according to the shape of their cells.

Fungi

Fungi can be further divided into two groups: **moulds** and **yeasts**. Food spoilage can be caused by mould and yeast, but harmless varieties of both are used in the production of various foods.

Bacteria

Bacteria are the most common source of food poisoning. They are found in the air, in water and in soil as well as in the intestines, mouths, noses and throats of animals, and on the surface of both plants and animals. They are the smallest of all single-celled micro-organisms.

Potent poison

In the right conditions, bacteria can reproduce very quickly through binary fission, a process in which one cell splits into two cells. This can take between ten and twenty minutes. Then, the two new cells each divide into two and so on. It is unlikely that just one bacterium will be present in some food in the first place, so it is easy to see how quickly bacteria can become a potential source of food poisoning.

Certain bacteria are known as **spore**-forming bacteria. Spores are hard, resistant bodies found within the bacterial cell and are able to withstand extreme conditions such as a very high temperature. When the conditions return to 'normal' the spores germinate, producing new bacterial cells and so the reproductive process starts again. *Bacillus cereus*, present in rice, is an example of spore-forming bacteria.

PORTORA LIBRARY

Conditions for growth

To grow, bacteria need food, moisture, warmth and time.

Food
Certain foods are known as 'high risk' because they are able to support the growth of bacteria. These foods include cooked and raw meat and poultry, shellfish, milk, eggs (and foods made from eggs) and cooked rice.

Moisture
If you look back to the 'high risk' foods you will notice they all have a fairly high moisture content. Bacteria are unable to survive in dry conditions (for example, in dried pasta, flour and powdered milk) because they need moisture to reproduce.

Warmth
Bacteria grow within a very wide temperature range (5–63°C). This is known as the temperature danger zone because if high risk foods are kept within this range for a period of time, bacteria will multiply rapidly. Most bacteria are killed at a temperature of at least 70°C.

Time
In only four or five hours, one bacterium can multiply into many thousand! This can be a particular problem at parties where buffet-style food is left out for long periods.

Yoghurt production

Beneficial bacteria

Yoghurt (fermented milk) is thought to have originated in the Balkans and Middle East. In Britain, yoghurt became popular during the 1960s when fruit yoghurts were introduced onto the market. Many yoghurt manufacturers market their products on the basis of the bacteria they contain. Yoghurts labelled 'probiotic' are made with **cultures** that are thought to aid digestion. The most common bacterial cultures used are *bifidus* and *acidophilus*, often referred to as 'friendly' bacteria because they are naturally present in the human gut and may help to breakdown food. Probiotic foods and drinks are known as **functional foods**.

Living bacteria

While only some yoghurts are labelled 'live', in fact all yoghurt contains living bacteria. The characteristic acidity and flavour of yoghurt is specifically due to *Lactobacillus bulgaricus* and *Streptococcus thermophilus*. These micro-organisms must be added in equal quantities otherwise the end result may be too bitter or too acidic. Natural yoghurt only contains milk and a **starter culture** but other ingredients can be added, such as powdered milk, evaporated milk, stabilizers, thickeners, fruit or fruit flavours, colouring and sugar. Low fat and very low fat yoghurts are also sold. Greek yoghurt has a higher fat content than other yoghurts but has become popular in recent years both as an ingredient and as an alternative to cream.

Production

Most of the yoghurt on sale in the UK is either 'stirred' or 'set'. Yoghurt is usually made from cows' milk but ewes' and goats' milk yoghurt are also available. The milk is **homogenized** to distribute the fat and then **pasteurized** (heated to 90℃ for 30 minutes) to kill all micro-organisms. The milk is then cooled to between 40℃ and 43℃ (the ideal temperature for the optimum growth of fermenting bacteria) and mixed with a starter culture. This inoculation process usually involves the addition of between 0.5 per cent and 2 per cent of *Lactobacillus bulgaricus* and *Streptococcus thermophilus*. As the bacteria multiply, the lactose (milk sugar) ferments, producing lactic acid and **diacetyl**, which gives yoghurt its characteristic flavour.

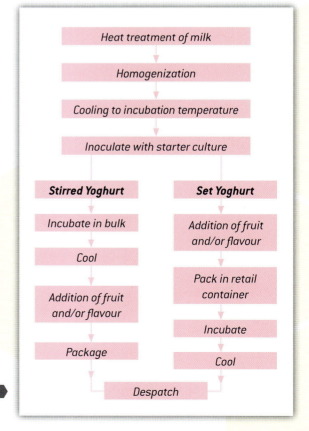

These are the stages in the production of stirred and set yoghurt.

Once a **pH** of 5.5 is achieved, conditions are ideal for the production of acetaldehyde (flavouring substance produced during fermentation), which also contributes to the yoghurt's flavour. The yoghurt is incubated for four to six hours at 32–37°C, depending on the type of yoghurt, during which time the proteins **coagulate** and the yoghurt thickens. The yoghurt is then cooled to 4.5°C.

Storage

Yoghurt must be stored below 5°C and eaten before the 'use by' date. If not, a fruit yoghurt for example, will continue to ferment and gas will cause the lid to 'blow' or bulge.

Yoghurt is an excellent example of the use of bacteria in food production.

Homemade yoghurt

Yoghurt can be made at home using a yoghurt-maker or vacuum flask.

You will need:
600ml pasteurized, sterilized, evaporated or UHT milk; 15ml spoon natural yoghurt; 50g dried skimmed milk powder (optional); kettle; vacuum flask that will hold at least 600ml; measuring jug; saucepan; tablespoon; thermometer

Method:
1 Boil water in the kettle and pour it into the flask, lid and measuring jug. Wash and dry the rest of the equipment thoroughly to prevent contamination of the yoghurt with micro-organisms.
2 Pour the milk into the saucepan. If it is pasteurized milk, bring it to the boil, then cool until the temperature reaches 43°C. There is no need to boil the treated milks, just heat to 43°C.
3 If using dried milk (which helps to thicken the yoghurt), add it to the warm milk. Also add the natural yoghurt and blend together. Pour the mixture into the measuring jug then, after draining the flask of water, fill the flask and put on the lid. Leave for about seven hours or overnight.
4 The following day pour the yoghurt into a very clean bowl and stand the bowl in a larger bowl filled with cold water. Stir the yoghurt gently. Once the yoghurt is completely cold, cover the bowl with clingfilm and put into the fridge for at least four hours. The yoghurt will thicken further in the fridge.
5 Serve the yoghurt plain on breakfast cereal, fruit or on desserts, or use it in recipes or as an alternative to cream. Items such as puréed fruit, jam, honey, nuts, oats and coconut can be added to your natural yoghurt.

Novel proteins

New ideas

Despite amazing advances in technology, there are still many areas of the world where food is in short supply. In addition, our total population is growing as people live longer and survive previously fatal diseases. For these reasons, scientists and food technologists have been working on the development of cheaper sources of protein known as **novel proteins**. **Micro-organisms** such as **yeast**, **fungi**, **bacteria** and algae have all been used as potential sources of cheap, edible protein. They are known as single cell proteins or biosynthesized proteins.

Other types of novel proteins have been produced by processing plant foods to make textured vegetable protein and textured soya protein. These products are also known as **smart foods**.

Cheap fermentation

Single cell proteins are grown through fermentation, a process similar to the one used in yoghurt and beer production. The micro-organisms are grown on a medium that contains a source of carbon, nitrogen and oxygen as well as water and small amounts of minerals (sulphur and phosphorus) and vitamins. The advantages of single cell proteins are that they can be grown in a cheap medium (such as waste carbohydrate material) and they grow very quickly.

Many forms of novel protein are produced so that they resemble meat in both texture and flavour. This is useful when they are used as 'meat extenders' (an added ingredient in meat to make it more economical), but this may not appeal to vegetarians who are trying to avoid eating meat-like products. Novel proteins are also described as meat substitutes or analogues.

Quorn™

Quorn™ is the trade name for a mycoprotein made from a mushroom-like plant called *Fusarium graminearum*. This fungi, which grows naturally in soil, was discovered in the early 1960s in a field near Marlow in Buckinghamshire.

Marlow Foods spent many years perfecting the production of Quorn™. The mycoprotein is grown in a fermenter (large sterile vessel). The fermenter is sealed and both the temperature and **pH** are carefully controlled. The nutrients (mentioned above) are pumped into the vessel and left for a few days to ferment. The mycoprotein then has to be separated from the liquid by pumping the mixture into a centrifuge, which spins out the liquid, leaving a creamy coloured dough. This mycoprotein is then heated to ensure the fermentation process is stopped.

In order to develop the texture of Quorn™, a series of processes are carried out, including mixing, steaming, chilling and freezing. These ensure the texture resembles the muscle fibres of meat. During this processing, vegetable flavours are added, as well as a small amount of egg white to bind the fibres together. The product is shaped and cooked, then chopped or minced ready for its end use.

Cooking with Quorn™

Quorn™ does not have much flavour of its own but is very good at absorbing flavours from other ingredients. The addition of spices, herbs and sauces or the use of a marinade all help to enhance the flavour of Quorn™ dishes. Unlike meat or chicken there is no waste because there is no bone, fat or skin to be removed. Quorn™ can also be cooked from frozen if necessary, but if not frozen it should be stored in a fridge.

Quorn™ contains a small amount of fat and no cholesterol. Unlike chicken, beef and tofu (a high protein product made from soyabean **curd**) it does contain **NSP** (non-starch polysaccharide), which is important for a healthy, balanced diet. Quorn™ is lower in energy value than both chicken and beef.

Facts about mycoprotein

Mycoprotein:

- is a fungus that contains high quality protein
- is naturally low in fat
- contains very few calories
- contains essential dietary fibre, which helps maintain a healthy digestive system
- is cholesterol free
- is completely meat free.

Adapted from Quorn's website www.quorn.co.uk

 The Quorn range includes chilled, frozen and ready meals.

Food spoilage

Going off

Food spoilage naturally occurs in all plants and animals after they have been harvested or slaughtered. Different foods result in different types of spoilage. For example, vegetables become soft and turn brown and meat develops a very unpleasant smell. This food may not be harmful but people are unlikely to want to eat it. The types of **micro-organism** that can cause food spoilage are **yeast**, **moulds** and **bacteria**.

Almost all of our food is produced by living organisms, whether they are animals or plants, and it is mainly composed of **organic** compounds. In the living plant or animal a variety of complex and carefully controlled reactions occur, mainly due to the presence of **enzymes**. Enzymes are proteins that speed up (catalyze) reactions. After harvest or slaughter, a whole series of reactions occur. For example, when fruit is picked it stops growing but it is still alive and ripening continues. Once the fruit is ripe, it will deteriorate rapidly (unless steps are taken to prevent this) due to the combined actions of enzymes and micro-organisms. Once harvested, the quality of fruit and vegetables declines due to a loss of water.

Most raw fruits (except those high in acid, such as grapefruit, oranges and lemons) darken when cut and exposed to the air. This discoloration of the surface is partly due to enzymes in the fruit coming into contact with the air. This effect is most noticeable in fruits such as apples and bananas. The reaction is called enzymic browning, and can be reduced by:

- removing the oxygen (for example, adding sugar syrup to fresh fruit salad)

 Bread may be covered with a green or blue mould.

- changing the acidity (for example, squeezing lemon juice over bananas)
- destroying the enzymes with heat (by **blanching** prior to freezing).

Speed of spoilage

All food spoils but the rate at which this process occurs depends on a number of factors. These factors are influenced by the nature of the food and the environment in which the food is kept. Meat is an example of a food that will spoil rapidly, and because of this it is regarded as highly perishable. Meat is normally sterile (free from living micro-organisms) until slaughter, when various types of contamination may occur. If meat is left untreated it will quickly deteriorate.

The perishable nature of meat is due to:
- the numerous nutrients it contains for micro-organisms to use
- its **pH**, which is within the range suitable for most micro-organisms to multiply

- the water content available for micro-organisms.

To reduce spoilage, all meat should be stored chilled, frozen or packaged using the **modified atmosphere packaging (MAP)** technique. Bacteria are mainly responsible for the spoilage of meat but moulds will grow if the conditions are right.

Protecting consumers

The loss of food through spoilage can have huge economic implications for the food industry. Although naturally spoiled food is not dangerous in terms of food poisoning, it is natural for consumers to avoid buying or eating it because it looks unattractive, and tastes and smells unpleasant. The food industry uses many preservation techniques in order to delay or prevent the deterioration of food.

Fresh fish

In recent years, researchers at the Norwegian Institute of Fisheries and Aquaculture Research have been working out a quick and easy method to determine the freshness of fish. Different species of fish have different keeping qualities, even with the same storage conditions. New technology uses a special device, called a spectrometer, to measure light at different wavelengths. Fish flesh absorbs light at different wavelengths, according to how it is stored and the length of time since it was caught. The spectrometer can determine the freshness of fish in just three seconds.

 Shiny skin is an indicator that fish like these sea bass are still fresh.

Micro-organisms

Amazing

Micro-organisms are amazing. They are tiny creatures invisible to the human eye and yet they are found almost everywhere on Earth. They play an essential role in all aspects of life; without **bacteria** most other animals would not be able to exist. However, they are also responsible for disease.

Classification

The characteristics of the five main types of micro-organism are listed below:

Algae – generally found in and around water, such as lakes, ponds, canals, rivers and oceans.

Protozoa – the largest micro-organism and therefore the first to be discovered; it can be found in many environments.

Fungi – includes **yeasts** and **moulds**; when present in sufficient quantity **fungi** can often be seen with the naked eye.

Viruses – do not require nutrients to grow but do need a **host**, in other words they are **parasites**. Human immunodeficiency virus (HIV) is a virus.

Bacteria – the largest group of micro-organisms; sometimes referred to as 'germs'; can be found virtually everywhere from human guts to soil.

Some classifications also include two additional groups.

- *Archaea* – similar to bacteria but can be found where no other creatures survive, such as in salt lakes or hot sulphur springs.
- *Sub-viral particles* – the smallest micro-organism known; one group is possibly responsible for the cattle disease **BSE**.

Fungi and bacteria are the most widespread micro-organisms and have the greatest impact on humans.

Fungi

Fungi require **organic** compounds for their survival. These may be in the form of dead organic material or living plants and animals. Some fungi, such as mushrooms, are recognizable, but others (moulds and yeasts) are microscopic. Moulds are multicellular because each mould consists of more than one cell. Moulds grow to produce a mass of branched, thread-like tubular structures called hyphae. These hyphae come from spores that are formed during reproduction, either inside a spore case or on their own. The spores then separate and travel in the air to find a suitable **substrate**. Some moulds are put to good use in the production of foods such as Danish Blue, Roquefort, Stilton and Camembert cheese.

Other moulds can cause food spoilage, even in food that is kept in the fridge. Most moulds are harmless, but some can cause disease. Certain moulds produce toxins (poisons) in food, known as mycotoxins.

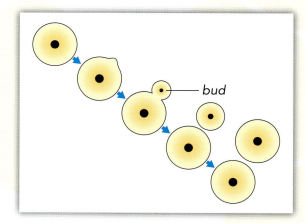

 Reproduction in yeasts is known as budding.

Yeasts are a form of fungi that grow on plant foods. Yeast can cause the spoilage of foods such as jam and meat, but other yeasts are essential in the production of bread, beer and wine. They are single-celled rather than multicellular and can be classified according to the shape of their cells — oval or rod-shaped. Like moulds, yeasts reproduce **asexually** in the process known as budding. Part of the yeast cell will slowly bulge out of the cell wall to create a 'bud'. The bud grows and eventually separates to form a new yeast cell.

Bacteria

Bacteria are the smallest single-celled micro-organisms. They can be divided into three groups according to the shape of their cells. Spherical cocci cells include food-poisoning bacteria such as *Staphylococcus aurus*. Rod-shaped bacilli cells include the bacteria *Bacillus cereus*, and vibrio cells (the short curved rod) include *Vibrio parahaemolyticus*. Both are also food-poisoning bacteria.

Bacteria multiply through binary fission. Put simply, this involves one cell dividing into two and this can happen in as little as ten minutes. Unlike fungi, bacterial cells have a nucleus, and

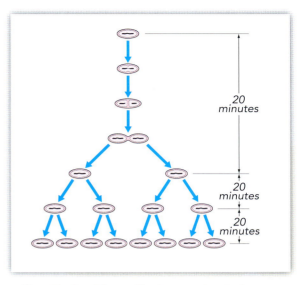

 During binary fission one bacterium can multiply to thousands in a few hours.

it is the nuclear material that is capable of reproducing itself, allowing the cell to become two distinct 'daughter' cells. The majority of food poisoning cases are due to bacteria and it is this ability to multiply so quickly (given the right conditions) that make bacteria so dangerous. For example, if a cream cake, which naturally contains some bacteria, is left in a warm place for a few hours, each bacteria will quickly multiply and soon the cake will be swarming with **pathogenic** bacteria.

 Certain moulds are essential in the production of cheeses such as Camembert, Stilton and Danish Blue.

Controlling micro-organisms

Ideal conditions

Food manufacturers and food processors can alter the environment in which food is packaged and stored in order to prevent or slow down the growth of **micro-organisms**. In order to do this, they must find out about the factors that affect the growth of micro-organisms. There are several conditions necessary and here, we will focus on the conditions needed for the growth of **bacteria**, as they are most likely to be the cause of food poisoning.

Time

Bacteria multiply by binary fission (see page 13). The time it takes bacteria to divide is called the generation time. Fortunately, they do not multiply at this rapid rate continuously. Scientists have discovered that there are four phases in the life cycle of a bacterial colony. The lag phase occurs at the beginning when no multiplication occurs; the log phase follows and involves rapid multiplication of bacteria; next the bacteria multiply and die off at about the same rate (known as the stationary phase) and finally, as bacteria run out of food and their waste products build up, bacteria gradually die in the decline phase.

Moisture

Like all organisms, micro-organisms need water in order to survive. For this reason, micro-organisms cannot grow in dried foods, such as flour and dried pasta, as long as these products are kept completely dry. The amount of moisture required by

micro-organisms varies and is described in terms of water activity (a_w). This describes the amount of water available to micro-organisms and can be illustrated with the examples in the table below.

Food	a_w	% Moisture
Pure water	1.00	100
Fresh meat	0.98	70.0
Bread	0.94	40.0
Flour	0.58	14.0
Sugar	0.19	0.2
Cream crackers	0.10	1.5

Bacteria usually need a source of food with a higher water activity than **yeasts** or **moulds**.

Food

Micro-organisms require **organic** substances, such as protein and carbohydrate, for food. Certain moist foods that have a high protein

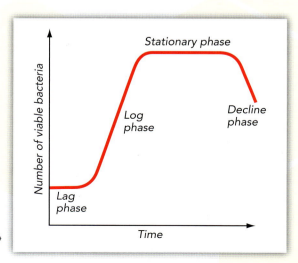

This graph shows the typical growth of bacteria.

High risk foods include poultry, eggs, milk and shellfish.

content provide ideal conditions for their reproduction. These foods are known as 'high risk foods' and they have been associated with 75 per cent of all cases of food poisoning. Moist, nutrient-rich foods include cooked meats, poultry, gravies, soups and stock, meat products, milk and milk products, eggs and egg products, shellfish and cooked rice.

Warmth

Each micro-organism has an optimum growth temperature, so a range of temperatures have been used to describe the 'temperature danger zone' of bacteria. Food poisoning bacteria multiply best between 5 and 63°C, so food must be kept outside this range. A fridge, for example, should operate below 5°C and when cooking, food should be held at 70°C for a sufficient length of time.

Take control

The growth of micro-organisms can be controlled in various ways:

1. *Food factors*
- pH – most fresh foods have a **pH** of around 7 (which is neutral) and micro-organisms grow best at this pH value. To prevent or slow down spoilage, foods can be made more acidic, for example during pickling.
- Available water – food is mainly composed of water, some of which is available to micro-organisms. By removing this moisture, or by adding substances such as sugar and salt, the water activity is decreased and foods can be kept longer. This principle is used in dried foods, salted foods (bacon) and preserves such as jam.

- Structure – some foods have a natural 'protection' such as a shell (nuts, eggs) or a skin (bananas, lychees) preventing the penetration of micro-organisms. However, once the outer covering is broken, spoilage and contamination can occur.

2. *Environmental factors*
- Temperature – storage temperature is very important when considering the growth of micro-organisms. Food may be stored in a warehouse, at home or in a supermarket. Room temperature is ideal for micro-organisms to multiply, unless they are otherwise controlled. Chilling, refrigerating and freezing slow growth and increase the shelf-life and safety of the food.
- Relative humidity – this is a measure of how much moisture there is in the atmosphere surrounding food. Dried foods, for example, must be packaged and stored to prevent them from absorbing moisture from the atmosphere.
- Oxygen – different types of micro-organism require different amounts of oxygen in order to multiply. Moulds are aerobic (need oxygen), while yeasts and bacteria can be either aerobic or anaerobic (do not need oxygen).

Making cheese

Cropwell Bishop Creamery

The Cropwell Bishop company dates back to 1847, although it has only been at its current site near Nottingham, since 1986. In addition to its main product, Blue Stilton, it also makes White Stilton, Shropshire Blue, and Stilton with added flavours such as apricot, pesto, ginger and citrus peel. The cheese is manufactured to the company's own high standards but in order to qualify as a Stilton, it must meet the regulations of the Stilton Cheese Makers Association.

Stilton cheese:

- was never actually made in the village of Stilton
- can only be made in one of seven licensed dairies in the world
- can only be made in the three counties of Derbyshire, Leicestershire and Nottinghamshire
- requires 78 litres of milk to make an 8 kilogram Stilton cheese.

Cropwell Bishop mainly supply to delicatessens and approximately 20 per cent of their cheese is exported all over the world. Exported cheese has to be carefully chosen to ensure it can withstand four or five weeks of travel.

Hats and coats

Everyone at Cropwell Bishop Creamery wears a hair net, hat, white coat and green Wellington boots (outdoors) or white Wellington boots (in the factory). Jewellery is not permitted and hands must be washed using knee-operated taps before entering the factory. An anti-bacterial gel is rubbed into the hands after washing. There is also a machine for washing the white boots, even though they do not actually leave the factory.

Helpful microbes

Every day fresh milk arrives in tankers at Cropwell Bishop's factory. The milk is stored, then **pasteurized** on the premises. The pasteurized milk is pumped into three open vats, each holding around 12,000 litres.

What's the difference?

Stilton	Cheddar
soft, creamy texture	firm texture
low volume starter culture	high volume starter culture
slow acidity build up	fast acidity build up
open vat production	closed vat production
packed into moulds, not pressed	packed into moulds and pressed
3–4 weeks to sell product	6 months to sell product

Rennet, a **starter culture** (containing **bacteria**) is added and for Blue Stilton, a **mould** *Penicillium roqueforti* is added to the milk which is kept at 30°C. The rennet is vegetarian and a non-genetically modified product. The low volume of this starter culture allows the acid to build up slowly during the long maturing process (compare with cheddar cheese – see box on page 16).

Dairy room

As the **curds** begin to form, cutters are used to break them up and the **whey** is gradually separated from the curds. (The fresh whey is used in the production of whey butter or fromage frais). The curds are then milled (chopped), salt is added and they are packed into plastic hoops of various sizes.

Handmade

In the hastening area, the hoops are turned by hand every day for five days as the curds gradually become more compact. Next, the hoops are removed and the cheese is 'rubbed up', which involves running a knife over the sides to seal it. Each cheese is labelled for

 Grading cheese is part of the process to ensure that the best quality cheese is produced.

identification and stored in the blueing rooms where they are turned twice a week. Gradually, a coat begins to develop on the outside of the cheese and the blue veins appear in the middle. After five weeks the cheese is ready for piercing to introduce air into the cheese so that the mould can reproduce, forming the distinctive blue veining. The piercing is repeated one week later.

Grading

Cropwell Bishop is a quality-orientated creamery. The quality of the cheese is assessed and maintained by the Quality Assurance Team. The Quality Assurance Manager is responsible for checking that the cheese-graders keep to a comparative standard when grading the cheese. Every cheese is individually graded twice.

A cheese iron is pushed in the side of the maturing cheese near the top, twisted, removed and replaced. This is then repeated near the bottom. The graders are looking for the degree of blue and the level of curd breakdown; a high level of breakdown means the cheese is soft and creamy. The graders also check the coat of the cheese for any defects.

Packaging

After the grading process, the cheese may be wrapped whole or cut into wedges and then wrapped. A whole cheese will be loosely wrapped in waxed paper, allowing it to breathe, before being boxed. The cut portions are more susceptible to contamination so they are shrink-wrapped in a breathable film. All cheese is labelled and dated, then stored at less than 5°C while it awaits transportation.

Food poisoning

Reported cases

Bacteria are responsible for the majority of reported food poisoning cases. It is quite amazing how something as minute as bacteria can cause such havoc with our health. Symptoms of food poisoning range from vomiting and diarrhoea to stomach pains, dizziness and headaches. In very severe cases food poisoning can be fatal.

Of course, it is difficult to tell just how many people actually experience food poisoning every year. Not everyone goes to their doctor when suffering sickness and diarrhoea, and it is only diagnosed cases that count in official statistics. However, it is clear that the incidence of food-related illness is on the increase. This may be due, in part, to a greater awareness of food poisoning but there are likely to be many other factors, such as changes in our lifestyle and the subsequent changes in how our food is prepared, from the farm to the dinner table. For example, the

- increase in intensive methods of rearing animals
- changes in type of animal feed used during rearing
- increase in food that has already been cooked or partly cooked for consumers
- trend in eating out more often and increase in variety of food outlets
- increase in bulk purchase of food
- move away from preservatives in food due to consumer pressure
- changes in the way people eat at home (for example, more microwave meals).

Food poisoning from bacteria can be divided into three categories:

1 Foodborne infections – cause illness through the presence of the multiplying organisms in the intestines. Examples include *Salmonella* species and *Listeria monocytogenes*.
2 Foodborne intoxications – cause illness through a toxin produced by the bacteria. Examples include *Staphylococcus aureus*, *Clostridium botulinum*, *Escherichia coli* (*E.coli*) and *Clostridium perfringens*.
3 Foodborne diseases – involve bacteria being transferred from one **host** to another via food. Examples include *Campylobacter jejuni*, *Salmonella typhi* and foodborne viruses.

Salmonella
There are various species of *Salmonella* so to indicate a variety of species, the abbreviated form is used (*Salmonella spp*). *Salmonella* account for the largest proportion of all reported cases of food poisoning. The reason for this is probably due to its incidence amongst large groups of people, such as at parties, schools and hospitals.

Listeria monocytogenes
These bacteria are found in the gut of animals and humans, in soil, sewage and throughout the environment. Unfortunately, they can grow at temperatures as low as 3°C so all foods associated with *Listeria* (soft cheeses, pâtés, raw meats, ice cream, prepared salads and chilled readymeals) must be stored correctly and eaten before their use-by date.

Staphylococcus aureus
These bacteria produce a toxin that is difficult to destroy with heat. As they live in our nose, mouth and in cuts and boils, it is important to observe high standards of personal hygiene at all times. Cooked meats, products containing cream and sandwiches have been associated with *Staphylococcus aureus* food poisoning.

Clostridium botulinum

There are several different types of this bacteria, all producing extremely heat-resistant **spores**. For food poisoning to occur, the spores must germinate and the organisms multiply in the food, producing a toxin. This has been associated with inadequately processed canned foods, fish and fish products.

E.coli 0157

E.coli 0157 is usually associated with poor personal hygiene because it is found in the bowels of people and animals, in sewage and in water. Its incidence has been rare but it can be particularly harmful to vulnerable people such as children and the elderly.

Clostridium perfringens

Another spore-forming bacterium that can cause poisoning if food is not cooled quickly enough or is inadequately reheated. It can occur when cooking large joints of meat, stews and gravies.

Campylobacter jejuni

A common cause of food poisoning, these bacteria are found in the guts of cattle, poultry, pigs, birds and pets. Cases tend to be sporadic (occur as a single incident rather than as an outbreak), so it is sometimes difficult to determine the source. However, raw (unpasteurized) milk, poultry and bottled milk pecked by birds have all been implicated.

 High standards of personal hygiene are essential during food preparation.

Contamination

Spreading germs

Food contamination is the presence of any unacceptable material in food from a 'fly in my soup' to the unseen presence of food poisoning **bacteria**. Many people think that bacteria are able to move independently and settle on food, but food has to come into contact with a contaminated source. Food can be contaminated directly, for example if a salad touches raw chicken before being served, or it can be indirect where an item, such as a dirty cloth, carries the bacteria. Contamination can be divided into three types: physical, chemical and biological.

Physical contamination

Any unwanted physical matter found in food is referred to as a foreign body. Foreign bodies include items that have come off equipment, such as nails, nuts and bolts, and paint flakes, and items that have fallen from food handlers, such as earrings, plasters and hair. Other types of physical contamination include cigarette ends, string and glass. Of course, any incidence of contamination like this shows a severe disregard to food hygiene and should be reported straight away, firstly to the manufacturer or shop owner and then perhaps to the local Environmental Health Office.

Some physical contamination can be prevented simply by keeping food covered at all times. This would stop flies and other insects landing on the food but it can also help stop contamination by **moulds** and **yeasts**. Mould **spores** are always present in the atmosphere, as are yeasts. It is important that kitchens are well ventilated as moulds grow more rapidly in damp environments.

Chemical contamination

It is quite ironic that the very things we use to clean equipment prior to food preparation may also contaminate our food! A whole array of cleaning agents and other substances, sometimes even dangerous chemicals, are used during food production. The contamination can occur at any point, from the spraying of pesticides while crops are growing, to anti-bacteria sprays on work surfaces. Chemical contamination can be a real problem because it can't generally be seen, although it may cause food to have a strange aroma. The resultant illness can be quite acute so the following basic rules should be kept to, both at home and within the food industry:

- Store chemicals well away from foods, preferably in a different area.
- To avoid confusion, never store chemicals in anything other than their original containers.
- Dispose of chemicals carefully and safely.

Good hygiene is essential in order to avoid food contamination.

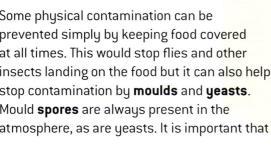

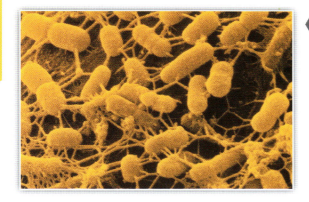

Contamination is always a risk. This is bacteria found on a used scrub pad.

animals and birds. This may include physical contamination if it involves something that can be physically seen in the food, but it can also involve contamination by defecation of insects, for example, within the food.

Biological contamination

Biological contamination can be divided into microbiological and non-microbiological contamination:

Microbiological contamination includes contamination by bacteria, moulds and viruses. This may occur due to the poor hygiene standards of food handlers or those in the premises.

Non-microbiological contamination includes contamination by insects, rodents, other

Vehicles

A vehicle is anything that can transfer bacteria from its source to a high-risk food. An example might be a knife that is used to cut raw meat and then to cut cooked meat without being washed between times. This is known as **cross-contamination**. Other examples include chopping boards, cloths and a food handler's hands. Bacterial contamination of foods can result in food poisoning.

Symptoms of food-related diseases

Bacterium	Onset time	Symptoms
Bacillus cereus	1 to 5 hours	Abdominal pain, vomiting and diarrhoea
Campylobacter	3 to 5 days	Abdominal pain, bloody diarrhoea, fever
Clostridium botulinum	12 to 36 hours	Difficulty swallowing and breathing, paralysis, often fatal
Clostridium perfringens	12 to 18 hours	Abdominal pain and diarrhoea
Escherichia coli	12 to 24 hours	Abdominal pain, diarrhoea
Listeria monocytogenes	3 days to 3 weeks	Contraction of meningitis and septicaemia, can be fatal
Salmonella	12 to 36 hours	Abdominal pain, diarrhoea, vomiting, fever
Staphylococcus aureus	1 to 6 hours	Abdominal pain, vomiting, diarrhoea

Hot and cold

Cooking food

All food handlers should be aware of temperature control during food preparation. The golden rule is to keep food either hot or cold and to keep it out of the 'temperature danger zone' as much as possible.

Sometimes, food is cooked but not eaten straight away. For example, if a meat curry is cooked at home but only half is eaten, the other half must be cooled as quickly as possible. It should then be wrapped and stored in the fridge until the following day or frozen. If the curry is cooled slowly, perhaps on the hob in a warm kitchen, **bacteria** will have the opportunity to multiply (warmth, moisture, time and food are all available).

This also applies in the food and catering industry – hot food must be kept hot and cold food kept cold, and if it needs to be cooled it must reach less than 10℃ within 90 minutes.

Probing temperatures

The thermometer pictured here shows that most bacteria are killed at 70℃. This is why it is essential that cooked food reaches at least 70℃ at its centre. Food must be held at this temperature for a sufficient length of time (which will depend on the type of food being cooked). It is important when checking temperature control that the core temperature is measured because this ensures the food is cooked throughout and not just at its edges. For this reason, some foods must be stirred during the cooking process. Temperature probes are used to test the core temperature of hot (and cold) foods.

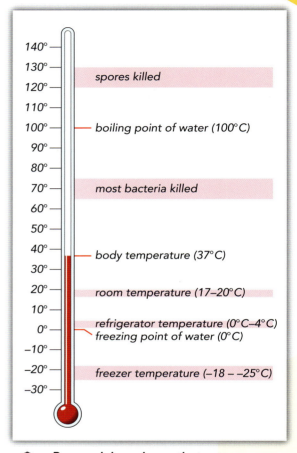

140°	
130°	
120°	spores killed
110°	
100°	boiling point of water (100°C)
90°	
80°	
70°	most bacteria killed
60°	
50°	
40°	
37°	body temperature (37°C)
30°	
20°	room temperature (17–20°C)
10°	
0°	refrigerator temperature (0°C–4°C)
	freezing point of water (0°C)
–10°	
–20°	freezer temperature (–18 – –25°C)
–30°	

 Research has shown that poor temperature control is responsible for the majority of cases of food poisoning.

High risk foods such as meat and poultry require extra thought during temperature control, for example a large joint of meat or a chicken containing a stuffing may not be sufficiently cooked in the centre. All meat must be thoroughly thawed before cooking, unless it has been specifically prepared for cooking from frozen.

Distributing bacteria

Bacteria are mainly found on the surface of meat, so minced or rolled meat needs extra care because the bacteria are distributed throughout the meat. This is why a burger with a slightly raw centre may pose a danger to health whereas a steak cooked rare (still pink in the middle) may not necessarily cause illness.

If food needs to be kept hot, perhaps during a hot buffet, it must be held at a temperature above 63°C (outside the temperature danger zone). Reheating food means heating it thoroughly so the centre reaches 70°C for at least two minutes. Microwave reheating can be a problem if consumers heat food so that it is just warm enough to eat rather than making sure it is piping hot. Food should not be reheated more than once.

Cold chill

A refrigerator or chiller should operate between 0 and 4°C and the temperature should be regularly monitored. Some bacteria can still multiply slowly within this temperature range so chilling should only be seen as short-term storage. Food should always be cold before it is put in a chiller otherwise the condensation created could cause **mould** growth.

Cook-chill systems involve food being rapidly chilled after cooking. This is often used for ready-meals sold in chiller cabinets. The cooked food must be chilled to less than 3°C within 90 minutes, and this is usually done using a blast-chiller.

Cook-chill food has a relatively short shelf-life because it can only be stored in a chiller or fridge for a maximum of five days. This includes both the day of production and the day it is eaten.

Cook-freeze systems of production are similar to cook-chill but the end product has a longer shelf-life – usually between two and twelve months. The reheating of both these foods must follow the guidelines mentioned above.

Frozen food

Freezing food controls the growth of micro-organisms in two ways. Firstly, water is no longer available and secondly the temperature is greatly reduced. Some foods (usually fruit and vegetables) are **blanched** before they are frozen as this prevents the activity of certain **enzymes** that cause browning. Some bacteria are also destroyed in the high temperatures of blanching.

There are four main methods of freezing:
1 Plate freezing – food passes between plates filled with **refrigerant**.
2 Immersion (or cryogenic) freezing – food is put directly into the refrigerant, which may be liquid nitrogen.
3 Blast freezing – food is subjected to blasts of extremely cold air.
4 Fluidized bed freezing – food (especially small-sized items such as peas) travels on a mesh through which extremely cold air is blown.

Heat treatment

Preserved food

Heat is used in cooking to make food both palatable and safe to eat. Food is also subjected to high temperatures in order to extend its shelf-life. This is known as preservation. Sterilization is a form of heat treatment that destroys all **micro-organisms** and their **spores**. Canning is a method of preservation that utilizes the process of sterilization. Foods can also be sterilized in glass bottles or jars (for example jam) and plastic containers (for example sterilized milk).

Canning

Canned food has a relatively long shelf-life, from a few months to several years, depending on the type of food. For this reason, canned foods make excellent ingredients for the 'store cupboard', although the high temperatures involved in the processing do affect the flavour and texture of the end product. Dented cans of food should never be used because there is a risk that **bacteria** may have entered and contaminated the contents. Cans are usually made from steel with a thin coating of tin but some containing foods high in acid also require a protective lacquer to prevent corrosion of the metal.

All kinds of foods can be preserved using the canning process but the system will vary according to the food. A basic canning process follows these steps:

1 The food is prepared as necessary (for example washed, peeled).
2 The food is cooked, partially cooked, **blanched** or left raw.
3 Each can is filled with a measured amount of food and air is removed.
4 Lids are sealed onto the cans using a hermetic (airtight) seal.
5 The food is sterilized in the can for the desired amount of time and to the correct temperature. These factors will depend on the size of the can and the type of food it contains. Acidic foods contain non-spore forming micro-organisms so will require a temperature of around 93°C, whereas non-acidic foods need higher temperatures (115–125°C) to ensure bacteria such as *Clostridium botulinum* and its spores are eliminated.
6 After cooling, cans may be stored at an **ambient** temperature.

Pasteurization

Since Louis Pasteur first discovered the process of **pasteurization** in the 19th century, many products other than milk have been found to be suitable for the process. Pasteurization reduces the number of harmful and spoilage micro-organisms to a safe level and is regarded as a short-term method of preserving food. Two forms of pasteurization are now used for a range of products including milk, cream, fruit juice, wine, beer and sauces.

The high temperature short time (HTST) method is usually used for milk and involves heating milk to 72°C for at least 15 seconds, then cooling it rapidly to 10°C. The holder process involves heating liquid to 65.6°C, holding it at this temperature for 30 minutes, and then cooling it rapidly to below 10°C.

UHT

The ultra heat treatment (UHT) process involves heating food to a high temperature for a very short time to kill all disease- and spoilage-causing micro-organisms. UHT foods can have a shelf-life of several months if they are unopened and correctly stored. They can be stored at ambient temperatures until they are opened and should then be treated as fresh. UHT is used with soups, sauces, beers, fruit juices, milk and milk products such as milkshakes. UHT milk is heated to 135°C for about one second. **Homogenized** milk is usually used. The effect of this processing on the flavour, colour and nutritional value of milk is minimal but it is more significant than the effects of pasteurization.

Special equipment

Heat treatment processes may be carried out using specialized equipment.

Plate heat exchanger – consists of many stainless steel plates sandwiched together with a heating and cooling medium flowing in opposite directions. The liquid flows from one side of the stainless steel plate to the other while being heated or cooled. The liquid does not come into direct contact with the heating or cooling medium.

Tubular heat exchanger – the liquid passes through stainless steel tubes that are surrounded by the heating or cooling medium.

Scraped surface heat exchanger – the liquid is pumped into a barrel, the walls of which contain the heating or cooling medium. Blades scrape the product from the walls ensuring the contents are evenly mixed. This type of equipment is used in making ice cream.

Footprints of milk

In the UK, about 93 per cent of milk consumed is fresh rather than UHT. However, with a growing concern about the impact of carbon emissions on the environment, some people suggest it would be better to use more UHT milk because it does not require refrigeration when unopened. A reduction in emissions and energy from manufacturers and retailers would help reduce our **carbon footprint**.

Heat treatment can be used with a range of milk products. All of these products have a longer shelf-life than fresh milk.

Dried foods

Sun-dried

Micro-organisms need moisture in order to grow and reproduce. The removal of moisture is known as dehydration and helps to preserve food. Leaving food in the sun to dry is one of the oldest methods of preservation.

Like freezing, dehydration does not kill micro-organisms but it does prevent them from growing. As soon as dried food absorbs moisture, the microbes can begin to reproduce again and the food must be treated as fresh.

Osmosis

If micro-organisms are present in food during dehydration, water will pass from their cells (a dilute solution) into the more concentrated solution surrounding them. Moisture leaves the cells of micro-organisms by a process called osmosis. Osmosis is the movement of water from a weak solution to a strong solution, through a semi-permeable membrane (see diagram). Once deprived of water, the micro-organisms cannot grow and some will be destroyed.

 Water moves from a weak solution to a strong solution by osmosis.

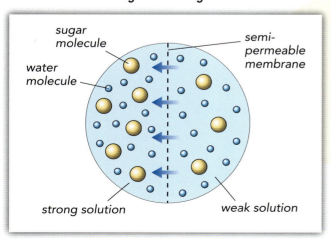

sugar molecule

water molecule

semi-permeable membrane

strong solution

weak solution

Food will remain dehydrated until water is put back (rehydrated), then the situation is reversed. Dried food must be stored in a cool, dry place to prevent any moisture being absorbed by the food. Unlike many other forms of preservation, drying does not require any special storage equipment for the food. Rice, flour, pasta and **pulses** are all examples of dried foods. Sea salt and spices are also sun-dried products. There is currently a consumer demand for 'ready-to-eat' dried fruit that does not require any soaking before it can be used. This is achieved by drying the fruit in the normal way but replacing sufficient moisture to give a moist texture without allowing the growth of micro-organisms. When water is removed from the cells of food, the concentration of sugars and salts increases, which affects the nutritional value of the end product (see box below right).

Drying methods

Sun drying is a traditional method of leaving food out in the sun and is still used today for some foods such as tomatoes and dried fruits.

Hot-air bed drying is used on solid foods such as meat. They are put onto perforated trays and hot air is blown through the trays under carefully controlled conditions (time and temperature).

Spray-drying is used for liquid foods such as milk. The food is blown as a fine spray into a hot air chamber where it dries and becomes granules. The granules then drop to the bottom for collection.

Roller drying is used for liquids such as milk. A film of liquid is picked up by a steam-heated roller. As the roller rotates the water evaporates leaving a dry film that is scraped off with a blade. This produces a finer powder that is easier than other dried foods to reconstitute.

Accelerated freeze-drying is used on liquid foods, such as coffee, which are rapidly frozen. Tiny ice crystals form in the food. These are quickly removed by turning them to vapour as the food is heated in a vacuum.

Additives

An anti-caking agent is added to some dry foods, such as salt and icing sugar, to help them flow freely. For example, E341, tri-calcium phosphate, is used for this reason. Other foods, such as confectionery and cake icing, have humectants added to prevent them from drying out and becoming hard. Humectants absorb water vapour from the air. An example is E420 (sorbitol).

 Dried foods tend to have a fairly long shelf-life.

Effects of drying

Colour: A food's colour may change completely through dehydration, for example green grapes become brown sultanas or currants. Food may darken because it becomes concentrated as it dries.

Texture: Food may become brittle (dried herbs), or it may become hard (dried pulses and peas), or it may crumble (coffee granules).

Appearance: Food may wrinkle, for example dried plums (prunes) shrink in size and become lighter in weight.

Flavour: Drying concentrates the food so flavours may become sweeter or saltier as a result. The heat may alter some of the characteristics of the food, for example the protein and carbohydrates, and therefore change the flavour, for example dried milk.

Nutritional value: Compared to fresh foods, this differs significantly in dried foods because when water is removed from the cells of food the concentration of sugars and salts increases. Dried food is a more concentrated source of energy. Water-soluble vitamins B and C are lost but once dried, nuts, fruits and vegetables are an excellent source of vitamins A and D as well as iron. Dried fruits are of particular importance as a source of iron to **vegans** and **ovo-lacto vegetarians**. Dried pulses are a good source of **low biological value protein** and **NSP**.

Personal hygiene

Taking it personally

Everyone has a responsibility to have a good standard of personal hygiene when they are preparing food. If the food is intended for friends or family the responsibility is a moral one. If it is as part of the catering or food industry then there is a legal obligation, as set out in the Food Safety (General Food Hygiene) Regulations 1995 (UK).

Personal hygiene is important because the body is actually a source of **micro-organisms**. Many types of **bacteria** live on the skin's surface and in its pores, as well as in the mouth, nose and ears. Bacteria are also present in the intestines, which is why it is crucial to wash hands thoroughly after going to the toilet.

Body parts

A lot of food preparation at home is carried out, quite rightly, by hand, for example in stuffing a chicken with sausage meat, folding filo pasty into samosas and kneading dough when making bread. Your hands naturally contain bacteria and they also pick up other bacteria during food preparation. Bacteria tend to lurk under the finger nails and beneath jewellery, so it is important to keep nails short and clean and remove all jewellery when cooking. The food and catering industry usually permit wedding rings (one plain band) to be worn but all other jewellery must be removed, including earrings and nose rings. For many tasks, food handlers are expected to wear disposable plastic gloves. Nail varnish must never be worn because it can chip and fall into the food.

Hand washing

Hands should be dried with disposable paper towels or using a blow-drier. Any cuts, grazes or sores should be covered with waterproof dressings that are changed regularly. These dressings are usually blue with a metallic strip inside so they can easily be detected should they fall into the food.

Hair may physically contaminate food. Hair, dandruff or hair accessories may fall out, and the bacteria *Staphylococcus aureus* may be present on hair, causing contamination. Hair must be kept clean and should never be brushed or combed when in a food area or while wearing protective clothing. All food handlers must wear hair nets and/or hats,

Hand washing is particularly important on certain occasions:
- after using the toilet
- on entering a food area
- before touching cooked food
- after coughing or sneezing
- after touching raw food
- after handling rubbish/waste
- after touching the face
- after dinner/tea break

 Hands should be washed regularly during food preparation, using hot water and soap, preferably liquid soap.

while nets must be used to cover beards. At home it is always a good idea to at least tie back long hair when preparing meals.

Staphylococcus aureus is also found in the nose, mouth, throat and ears and may be transferred to food through coughing, sneezing, picking the nose and so on. Food handlers should never dip their fingers into food to taste it or lick their fingers when opening plastic bags. Anyone suffering from a bad cold or influenza should not work with food. Smoking is against the law in a food preparation area.

Protective clothing

In addition to protective headwear, food handlers must wear protective clothing such as an overall or an apron. These must be clean and fastened securely. Generally, such clothing does not have pockets where food

might accumulate and cuffs are elasticated to prevent anything falling into the food. Some overalls and aprons are disposable and some are colour-coded according to the task being carried out.

Footwear needs to be comfortable and non-slip in a food environment. In factories where areas might be wet, rubber boots are often chosen for both safety and protection.

Feeling ill

As a food handler, it is important to report any illness to a supervisor or someone in authority. In particular, if suffering from a stomach upset, a cold, an eye or ear infection or food poisoning symptoms, it is likely you will be told you cannot work. If you have to visit your doctor with any of these illnesses, inform your doctor that you work with food.

Food handlers must wear clean, protective clothing to avoid any cross-contamination.

Kitchen layout

What is a food premise?

When someone decides to set up a food business, whether it is a factory making tins of baby food or a take-away fish and chip shop, they need to find suitable premises. Food premises are defined in the Food Safety Act 1990 as being anywhere that food is prepared, stored or sold and, as well as the two obvious examples above, this includes farms, market stalls, ships and aircraft. Unless a business operates for less than five days in a five-week period, it must be registered with the Local Authority and it will receive visits from the local Environmental Health Officer (see page 40).

Where to operate

Choosing an appropriate location for a food business can be difficult as there are many aspects that need to be considered. Retail businesses must, of course, consider location in terms of how accessible it is for their customers, but here we will focus on the location of manufacturing outlets in terms of health and safety.

Clearly it would not be a good idea to locate a food manufacturing business in the same area as a building that creates dust, fumes or odours. **Mould spores** from cereals can travel in the air so a location away from farms is also advisable. Nobody wants to run the risk of

 Different foods are prepared in different areas to avoid the risk of contamination.

flooding by locating close to water, but rivers and streams can also provide a source of pests for food manufacturers.

There may also be reasons why other people do not want a food factory close by! Food manufacturers can create their own kinds of noises and smells and the transportation of products and materials can cause problems for local people, especially if the factory operates 24 hours a day.

Factory layout

Well-designed premises will ensure that all materials pass quickly and easily from one stage of production to the next. They should also be handled as little as possible. Both these factors help to reduce the risks of their contamination, damage and deterioration. All materials arriving at the manufacturers (raw materials and packaging materials) are inspected and stored in their appropriate area (for example, a refrigerator store, a freezer store or a dry store). They should not come into contact with anything in the food processing area.

Any effluent (outflow of liquid waste such as sewage) from the factory should drain away from buildings, storage and production areas. All drains and gutters should be kept free-flowing to avoid any blockages leading to a back-flow of waste materials. The building itself must also be secure from pests (as well as people) and be regularly maintained to ensure against leaks or the deterioration of the building.

Kitchen layout

The following should be considered when designing the layout of a kitchen:
- The workflow in any kitchen area must be a smooth operation. It should be well organized and avoid time wastage by having items sensibly stored according to their end use. The workflow should pass smoothly from delivery to storage to preparation to service/packaging.
- For reasons of hygiene, certain foods need to be treated separately. For example, vegetables and fruit may have soil on them so should be confined to one area, while raw meat and poultry should be kept in another area to avoid **cross-contamination** (see page 20).
- Most commercial kitchens now contain stainless steel or other non-porous materials. Wood should be avoided as a work surface, cupboard or chopping board because **bacteria** can lodge in cracks and wood absorbs liquids.
- Food preparation areas must have toilets and washing facilities. Toilets must not lead directly onto food rooms. Hand-wash basins must be provided. Within the food area itself, hand-wash basins should be provided separately from the sinks used to wash and prepare food items.
- Good ventilation is essential when working with food as it removes steam, heat, condensation and odours. Remember: bacteria enjoy moist, warm environments!
- Walls and ceilings should be light coloured so any splashes of food or grease will show up easily. They should be as smooth as possible to prevent the harbouring of dirt and bacteria. Floors must be non-slip and easy-to-clean. Many kitchens contain equipment on wheels so it can be moved and the floor underneath cleaned.
- A well-lit area is essential for food preparation – both in industry and at home! This is partly for the food handlers' own safety but also to ensure food is being prepared hygienically.

Risk assessment

Risky business

The way food hygiene is managed in all areas of the industry involves a straight forward and sensible approach. Before the 1990 Food Safety Act was passed, problems associated with poor hygiene were only corrected after something had gone wrong, for example after someone had complained of food poisoning. However, today's approach is **proactive**. It involves identifying any possible hazards first, assessing the degree of risk and then implementing systems to reduce the risk to a safe level. This approach is known as risk assessment.

Assessing risks

Risk assessment can be defined as a method of identifying risk factors (hazards) and judging how likely it is that a hazard will occur. In the food industry this means anything that has the potential to harm the consumer. Hazards can be categorized as microbiological (for example **micro-organisms**), chemical (for example cleaning agents) and physical (for example foreign bodies). The consequences of these are food-related illnesses, an injury through consuming food containing a foreign body, and/or the spoilage of food. Potential hazards may come from a variety of sources including equipment, food handlers, food products, the environment and production processes. Hazards can occur at any stage of food processing, from primary processing, such as the use of insecticides on crops, to secondary processing, such as in the preparation of a meat pie filling, as well as all the stages in-between, such as during transportation, storage, distribution and consumer use.

Why bother?

Anyone involved in the food and catering business has both a legal and a moral responsibility to ensure the food being prepared and sold is fit for consumption. Studies have shown that production processes and the state of cleanliness directly affect the chances of food poisoning occurring. It has already been stated that poor temperature control is one of the most important causes of food poisoning. Listed below are some of the main factors identified in food poisoning cases. Of course, more than one of the following may be involved in a single case.

- Food prepared too far in advance
- Food stored at room temperature
- Food cooled too slowly
- Food not reheated properly
- Use of precooked food containing food poisoning organisms
- Food undercooked
- Use of contaminated canned food
- Food inadequately thawed before cooking

 Risk factors can occur at any point during processing, from crop spraying to packaging the final product.

- **Cross-contamination** allowed to occur
- Raw food consumed (for example raw eggs, raw shellfish).

Rotating stock

One method of control used by the food and catering industries is the principle of stock rotation. This very simple idea should also be put into practice by consumers as it helps to prevent using out-of-date foods by mistake. When new stock is being stored, it should be put to the back and stock with an earlier datemark brought to the front so that it is used first. This applies to **ambient**, chiller and freezer storage.

Hygiene systems

By following safe and hygienic systems for producing food, all those involved in food businesses can be confident they are doing all they can to produce safe food all the time. One such system is HACCP (Hazard Analysis Critical Control Points). This technique is widely accepted and used within the food industry. Another system, ASC (Assured Safe Catering), is based on the HACCP system but has been developed by the Department of Health specifically for the catering industry. A separate system was thought to be necessary because not all catering operations have the resources to implement HACCP.

ASC involves looking ahead to consider any problems that might occur in production and putting procedures into place to stop them occurring. For example, during the service of a hot buffet, food must be kept above 63°C. The equipment used to keep it hot must reach that temperature before food is placed inside. If this fact is established before production begins, a potential problem will be swiftly eliminated.

Accurate temperature control is essential during the service of a hot buffet.

Systems of hygiene

Food in space

Strange as it may sound, HACCP (Hazard Analysis Critical Control Point) was a system developed in the 1960s to produce safe food for astronauts. The aim was to provide perfectly safe food, which is fairly important when you are floating around in space! The system was effective and has been taken up by the food industry as a method of ensuring food is produced safely and hygienically. The following information about the HACCP system can also be applied to the ASC (Assured Safe Catering) system.

During the process of HACCP, a product, or group of very similar products, are analysed to assess hazards that may be associated with the product, the production process, the equipment, the environment and the staff involved. Once all hazards have been identified, the level of risk is considered and critical control points (CCPs) are developed. A CCP is a step in a food production system where control is essential to eliminate a hazard or reduce it to a safe level and therefore guarantee food safety. A CCP might be a temperature achieved during heat treatment (for example 72°C) or chilling (for example 2°C). These temperatures will have a tolerance value, which means they take into account the fact that the temperature could be just above or just below that temperature. So, in fact, the temperature during heat treatment could be between 70°C and 74°C and this would still be acceptable. The tolerance value would be said to be +/− 2°C (72°C +/− 2°C).

Checking up

Clearly, it is not enough to simply state the temperature within a HACCP system. There has to be a means of monitoring and controlling what goes on. Using the example

 A food probe is used to monitor the temperature of food.

of temperature control once again, the temperature could be controlled using a computerized heating system, and checks made on a regular basis to monitor that everything is working properly. The checks can be made with a temperature probe and the charts completed would become an important part of the HACCP system. Other important records that would be needed include cleaning schedules, delivery checks, maintenance of equipment, pest control and the temperature checks of items such as refrigerators, chillers and freezers.

Taking control

Every food business needs to ensure that everything that can be controlled is controlled throughout the production process. These controls might include:

- ensuring staff are adequately trained in appropriate aspects of hygiene
- only buying from reputable suppliers
- using efficient stock rotation methods
- storing food correctly at all times
- keeping raw and cooked foods apart at all times
- cooking food to the correct temperature and for the correct length of time
- keeping hot food at the correct temperature
- chilling/freezing food to the correct temperature
- enforcing adequate cleaning systems
- enforcing adequate pest control.

Within the HACCP system, monitoring involves observing or measuring aspects of the production process. Monitoring is essential to ensure CCPs are being controlled. Monitoring often involves visual checks, for example looking at raw ingredients on their arrival or checking date marks after food has been packaged.

HACCP steps

Any food business can use the HACCP system. These are the basic steps to be followed:

1 Hazard analysis: the production process is broken down into a series of steps (perhaps as a flow chart) and any hazards are listed.
2 Critical control points: suitable CCPs are identified.
3 Critical limits: critical times and temperatures for each CCP must be identified and tolerance levels set.
4 Monitoring: methods of monitoring each CCP must be devised.
5 Record keeping: decisions need to be made about recording the monitoring.

If the monitoring indicates that a problem has occurred, any food affected will need to be removed and action must be taken to correct the problem. It is also important to have an overall checking procedure to ensure the system is working effectively.

Hazard a go

See if you can design your own HACCP system by listing all the steps involved in making your favourite recipe. Present your list in the form of a flow chart and, using a different colour pen, write down a potential hazard that may occur (such as **cross-contamination**). Next, using a third colour, write down the control point needed to ensure each potential hazard doesn't occur (for example use different chopping boards for meat and vegetables). Finally, state how you could monitor your critical control points.

Factory hygiene

Clutter free

Maintaining high standards of hygiene in a food factory is not easy. A factory may be working 24 hours a day with an output of massive quantities of food. However, hygiene is of the utmost importance and the following guidance can help to achieve high standards.

In an environment that may be full of people, equipment and even vehicles, it is necessary to keep all processing and storage areas clean and tidy. Floors will need washing or, where dry conditions are required, vacuum cleaning on a regular basis. Walls and ceilings must also be kept free from any dirt or food residue, especially if conditions are moist and so would encourage the growth of **bacteria**. Ideally, food factories should not contain any surfaces where dirt or food can accumulate, for example window sills or shelves. Any drains within a factory must be regularly cleaned, and capped when not in use.

Moving plants

Manufacturing machinery is known as 'plant' and it may be fixed or portable. Obviously, it is easier to maintain the cleanliness of portable plant and equipment, and the area underneath is more accessible too. Whether fixed or portable, plant and equipment should not be left for long periods without being cleaned and, if appropriate, should be disinfected.

Breaking barriers

Food factories generally function by having separate processing areas. For example, raw ingredients are kept separate from cooked products and so are dealt with in different areas. Often, food workers are restricted to certain areas in a system known as 'barrier hygiene'. Those working in the packing area, for example, will not be allowed to enter an area where salad ingredients are being prepared. These two sets of workers will have to wear different types of protective clothing that may be colour-coded.

 All equipment must be cleaned thoroughly on a regular basis.

Cleaning agents

Cleaning agents can be classified as detergents, disinfectants and heat. Detergents are used to remove any solid matter or food residue. A washing-up liquid is an example of a detergent. Detergents do not kill bacteria on their own. Disinfectants are chemicals that are designed to destroy bacteria and reduce it to a safe level. Food businesses often use disinfectants known as sanitizers, which contain both chlorine-based and iodine-based compounds. Used on their own, disinfectants will not usually remove dirt or food particles. Heat is, of course, involved in many cleaning procedures. Hand-washing needs to be done using hot water and a detergent. Heat alone can clean if it is either hot enough or powerful enough. High temperatures kill bacteria and steam can be used to steam-clean equipment and areas such as floors.

Cleaning methods

Several cleaning methods are used in food factories as different types of cleaning are required for different occasions.

Clean-as-you-go
The 'clean-as-you-go' system needs to be done all the time. It is necessary to clean work surfaces, equipment and yourself during food preparation to avoid **cross-contamination** and to ensure the work area remains clean and tidy. As part of the system all waste must be disposed of immediately and appropriately.

Wet and dry
Wet cleaning involves water and a cleaning agent and perhaps rinsing, too, either before or after cleaning. Any plant or equipment that has been wet-cleaned must be dried thoroughly to avoid creating the right conditions for bacterial growth. Dry cleaning involves the use of brushes and vacuum cleaners and may be necessary where powdered food is used. Cleaning agents are not used with this method so the cleanliness of the brushes and other equipment is vital.

On schedule
Scheduled cleaning is cleaning that needs to be done at regular intervals. Factories should have their scheduled cleaning tasks clearly written out with what needs to be cleaned, how it is to be done, who will complete the work, how often it is to be done, and the protective clothing that should be worn. Fixed plant and equipment will be 'cleaned-in-place', perhaps using spray chemicals and thorough rinsing. The process may be computer controlled, ensuring the right strength of cleaning chemicals. Portable plant and equipment can be moved and/or dismantled so it is said to be 'cleaned-out-of-place'. This is usually carried out by hand.

Home cleaning

The use of many anti-bacterial cleaning agents can lead some consumers to become complacent about cleaning as they believe everything will be hygienic after a squirt of anti-bacterial spray. However, many consumers are concerned about the use of chemicals in cleaning products and the effect of these on the environment. The best defence against cross-contamination is thorough and regular cleaning using hot water and detergent.

Possible pests

Pest control

Animals, insects and birds are all a potential source of food contamination. Buildings should be sufficiently secure to prevent pests entering, and the premises and stock should be checked regularly for signs of **infestation**. Common food pests in this country include:

- rodents: rats and mice
- insects: flies, wasps, ants, cockroaches, silverfish, weevils
- birds: pigeons, magpies, sparrows.

All pests like food, warmth and shelter, and food premises can provide all of these! To prevent pests from entering in the first place, all deliveries should be thoroughly checked and, where doors and windows do open, fly screens should be used if possible. Food materials should never be stored on the floor and, if necessary, foods should be emptied into pest-proof containers.

Avoiding temptation

As it is difficult to ensure pests do not enter a food area, it is important to discourage them if they do get in. All food spillages, especially crumbs, should be cleared up immediately whether on the work surface or floor. Adopt the procedure of 'clean-as-you-go', which includes the washing of equipment after use. Bins should be emptied regularly during the day and again at the end of the day. Regularly clean out storage areas to ensure there are no spillages or broken packaging.

Rodents

Mice and rats can be a particular problem in food premises because they breed quickly. Tell-tale signs include droppings, fur, urine stains and nibbled packaging. Rats also tend to follow a set pattern of movement so that eventually these 'runs' may be seen on the floor or walls. Mice are able to get through surprisingly small spaces. The control of rodent infestations usually requires using specialized treatment including baits, rodenticides (rodent poison) and traps.

Insects

If a housefly lands on your food it will feed by regurgitating onto the food, then sucking up the partly-digested material, and it will probably defecate (urinate and discharge faeces) at the same time! Flies do not mind where they get their food from so before landing on your food a fly may have fed from some rubbish in the street. This provides a pretty convincing argument for keeping flies out of the kitchen!

 Mice and rats are a potential source of contamination.

mouse

rat

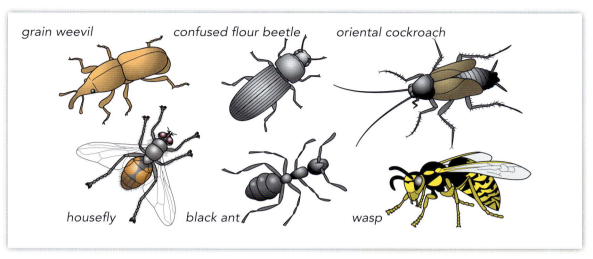

grain weevil confused flour beetle oriental cockroach

housefly black ant wasp

 Insects are attracted by the same foods we like to eat! They should not be allowed access to food areas.

Fly screens on windows and doors and self-closing doors are effective deterrents. Insect killers such as ultra-violet lights deal with insects if they do get in but they must be carefully located and cleaned out regularly.

Ants can be a problem, particularly in the summer months. They tend to be attracted by sweet foods. Specialist treatment may be needed to destroy their nest, which may be difficult to locate.

Cockroaches are not easy to spot for two reasons: they only come out at night and the rest of the time they lurk behind cupboards and in drains. They carry the **bacteria** *Salmonella* and *Staphylococcus aureus*. Cockroaches are likely to gain access through the delivery of goods so, again, thorough checking is essential. Weevils are one of a group of insects that physically contaminate dried foods such as flour. It is advisable to remove dried foods from their packet and to record their best-before date. Weevils can be seen with the naked eye, so always look carefully at flour before using it.

Birds

Wild pigeons, sparrows and magpies are not likely to get into food premises very often and they will be noticed if they do! However, they can contaminate food with their droppings and feathers so they should be removed as quickly as possible. To avoid a repeat visit, their means of entry should be discovered and blocked.

Pest control training

All food handlers should be trained regarding pest control so that they know what to look for and where to report their findings. The sort of things to look for include droppings, teeth marks on food or little piles of food gathered together, nibbled packaging, dirty trails on the floor or walls, unusual smells and pest carcasses.

The principles of stock rotation discussed on page 33 are also important in the prevention of pests.

A day in the life of an EHO

EHO

An Environmental Health Officer (EHO) is required to enforce various acts of law, including the Food Safety Act 1990. An EHO is entitled to enter a business. The business must co-operate with an EHO, and make changes to the premises or methods of food preparation in order to comply with the law. Food or other substances can be removed by the EHO and taken away for analysis. The following illustrates the sort of events that are 'all in a day's work' for Linda Haywood, an Environmental Health Officer in Sheffield.

A fishy start

9 am A quick check of the in-tray reveals a complaint about a fish and chip shop. Someone was seen smoking in the service area and it was reported that they did not wash their hands before serving, while the back of the shop looked dirty and untidy. Linda first contacts the complainant and obtains a description of the 'smoker', then schedules a visit to the shop the following day.

Next, a suspected food poisoning case. Linda contacts the complainant who explains that the day after eating at a local restaurant they suffered vomiting and diarrhoea. Linda needs confirmation that it is food poisoning and not a virus, so tells the complainant to visit their doctor to discuss symptoms and submit a faecal (stool) specimen for analysis. This is the only way to prove food poisoning **bacteria** are present. Details of all foods eaten and the time of onset symptoms are taken from the complainant and Linda suggests that all those present at the meal are contacted to see if they are suffering any illness.

Sandwich time

10 am After consulting her list of premises due for a routine food safety inspection, Linda sets off to visit a sandwich shop. A full hygiene inspection is carried out which starts with an interview of the shop owner. Hazard analysis and critical control points (HACCP) that are currently followed are discussed as well as all stages of food production, including buying foods in, storage, preparation, cooking and cooling, through to the display and service of the food. Advice is offered with regard to temperature control, record keeping and monitoring of temperatures.

Linda then inspects the premises, checking for cleanliness, structural defects, signs of pests, etc. She checks food using a probe thermometer. These findings are then discussed with the proprietor. A full report is to be sent following the inspection.

1 pm Back in the office, and after a snatched lunch that includes dealing with a variety of telephone queries, Linda gets on with the inspection report for the sandwich shop.

Mice drop in …

6 pm Unfortunately, some inspection visits have to be made during the evening because not all food outlets have daytime opening hours. Today involves one such visit so Linda and a colleague travel to a Chinese takeaway in their district. The visit is just one of their routine General Food Hygiene inspections, although what they find is not at all routine. The takeaway quite clearly has an **infestation** of mice (droppings are visible on the floor, in the food preparation area, in the food and even in the fridge). This case calls for a serious response from the Environmental Health Inspectors. Despite customers arriving to order or collect their takeaway for the evening, Linda has to serve an Emergency Prohibition Notice on the owners who must close the premises straight away. The notice must also be displayed for customers to see.

Evidence has to be collected so that a prosecution file can be put together. Notes are made and photographs are taken to record every detail of the state of the premises. Legally, an EHO team have two days to put together a file and they must apply to the court for a Prohibition Notice on the third day. So, the next day's work is already mapped out.

Getting qualified

To become an EHO in the UK it is necessary to follow a course that has been accredited by the Chartered Institute of Environmental Health (CIEH). School leavers will typically need 160 UCAS points with science at AS/A2 level, or 200 UCAS points without science. Alternatively, entry can be gained through an appropriate GNVQ, BTEC or Foundation Degree qualification. The course is usually a four-year sandwich course, which includes a year of practical training experience. EHOs are employed by Local Authorities, the Army, Navy and Air Force as well as the private sector.

An Environmental Health Officer enforces food regulations.

Hygiene law

Fit food

It is necessary to have laws that protect the public against food being sold when it is unfit to eat. The main legislation relating to the sale of food for human consumption in the UK is the Food Safety Act 1990. It aims to:

- protect consumers against food that may harm them
- prevent food that is not of a satisfactory quality from being sold
- prevent food from being labelled or described inaccurately.

There are four main offences within these areas of the Food Safety Act. It is an offence to:

- make food harmful (or injurious) to health
- sell food which does not meet food safety requirements
- sell food which is not of the 'nature, substance or quality demanded' by consumers
- incorrectly label, describe or advertise food.

At a local level the Food Safety Act is enforced by Environmental Health Officers. If someone is taken to court for an offence committed under the Act, a penalty of two years imprisonment and/or a maximum fine of £20,000 is possible. However, a defendant is allowed to show that all reasonable precautions were taken by providing evidence of the hazard analysis and risk assessment systems that were in place at the time. This is known as the defence of due diligence.

Regulations

When the food law was updated to produce the Food Safety Act, government ministers were given the freedom to produce regulations and orders that are legally binding. This is necessary due to the rapidly changing nature of our food today, particularly regarding food scares such as **BSE**. We also now need to comply with aspects of European directives and this can be done within the scope of Food Regulations.

New food hygiene laws have been in place since the beginning of 2006. The Food Hygiene (England) Regulations 2006 provide the basis for the European Union (EU) legislation that is in place in England. Wales, Scotland and Northern Ireland have similar regulations.

This legislation has simplified the law and makes it clear that it is the primary responsibility of food business operators to produce food safely.

Hygiene certificates

A number of organizations, such as The Royal Society for the Promotion of Health, now offer a certificate in basic hygiene and all food handlers should be encouraged by their employers to follow the course. The training can be done in a day and is appropriate for anyone who handles food, from serving in a bread shop to waiting on tables.

Scary food

There appears to be a growing number of stories about the harmful effects of certain foods. Does salmon cause cancer? Will chicken give you avian flu? Check out any concerns you may have. Use the internet and sites such as www.foodstandards.gov.uk.

Controlled temperatures

The Food Hygiene (England) Regulations 2006 also address the control of temperature for everything from raw materials to the storage of the end product. These regulations state that food must be below 8°C or above 63°C. This is slightly confusing because the temperature danger zone is between 5°C and 63°C. Although the risk of keeping foods at 8°C rather than 5°C is only small, it is still advisable to have chilled food between 0°C and 4°C.

Marking dates

As part of the Food Labelling Regulations 1996, all highly perishable foods must carry a 'use-by' date and it is an offence to sell the food after that date. Most other food has a 'best-before' date, which means the food will be at its best until that date. After this time the food will not be harmful but may not be at its best. It is not an offence to sell food after its best-before date unless it is stale or has an unpleasant taste or smell. Only the person responsible for date-marking a food is allowed, by law, to alter the date, although they may give their written permission for someone else to do so. Foods sold loose or without packaging are not required by law to carry a date-mark. This includes meat from a butcher, fish from a fishmonger, and fresh fruit and vegetables.

 This woman is maintaining hygienic working practices by covering her hair and wearing gloves while cooking.

Resources

Books

Create! Food Technology Student Book, Barbara Motteshead (Heinemann Educational Publishers, 2003)

Essential Food Hygiene (3rd edition), Dr R. J. Donaldson OBE (The Royal Society for the Promotion of Health, 1999)

Food Hygiene for the Food Industry, Dr R. J. Donaldson OBE and R. Early MSc FIFST (The Royal Society for Health, 2004)

Food Safety, Victoria Sherrow (Chelsea House Publishers, 2007)

GCSE Design and Technology for AQA: Food Technology Student Book, Lesley Woods (Heinemann Educational Publishers, 2005)

Making Healthy Food Choices (series) (Heinemann Library, 2006)

Oxford Dictionary of Food and Nutrition (2nd edition), David A. Bender (Oxford University Press, 2005)

The Essentials of Design and Technology: Food Technology, Janet Inglis (Lonsdale Revision Guides, 2002)

The Foundation HACCP Handbook (2nd edition), Richard Sprenger (Highfield Publications, 2005)

Websites

www.eatwell.gov.uk
This site provides the latest news from the Government's Food Standards Agency relating to food and health. Topics include healthy diet, keeping food safe, food labels and health issues.

www.foodforum.org.uk
This site is aimed at students as well as teachers and gives a good overview of food technology.

www.foodstandards.gov.uk
The Government's information website for the Food Standards Agency contains details of their aims, research, committees, regulations, press releases, etc. It also addresses topical issues such as food labelling and packaging.

www.rsph.org
The Royal Society for the Promotion of Health is a public health organization that provides information and publications as well as acting as an examining body for qualifications in food hygiene and safety.

Contacts

British Nutrition Foundation
High Holborn House
52–54 High Holborn
London
WC1V 6RQ
Tel: 020 7404 6504
www.nutrition.org.uk

The Food & Drink Industry National Training Organisation
6 Catherine Street
London
WC2 5JJ
Tel: 020 7836 2460
www.foodanddrinknto.org.uk
More information on training and careers in food and drink manufacturing.

Institute of Food Science & Technology
5 Cambridge Court
210 Shepherd's Bush Road
London
W6 7NJ
Tel: 020 7603 6316
www.ifst.org
Gives information on food-related training and careers.

Sustain (previously The National Food Alliance)
94 White Lion Street
London
N1 9PF
Tel: 020 7837 1228
www.sustainweb.org
Publications focus on food and its production, looking at how food is grown, manufactured, transported and stored.

SNAGS – School Nutrition Action Groups
Health Education Trust
18 High Street
Broom
Alcester
Worcs
B50 4HJ
Tel: 01789 773915
The aim of SNAGS is to increase the uptake of a healthier diet by supporting education and health professionals to improve the range of food and drink provided in their schools.

Glossary

ambient   refers to a temperature. Ambient foods are found on supermarket shelves rather than in temperature-controlled cabinets such as a chiller or freezer. Ambient foods include tinned products, UHT products and dried products.

asexually   without sex; reproduction that occurs asexually does not require a male and female in order for it to take place

bacteria   type of micro-organism; often classified according to their shape and whether they reproduce aerobically or anaerobically or both. Harmful bacteria can cause food poisoning while harmless bacteria aid in the production of some food products.

blanching   immersing food in boiling water very briefly before cooling it rapidly. It destroys enzymes that cause browning in vegetables.

BSE (bovine spongiform encephalopathy) also known as 'mad cow disease'. A disease transmitted from animals to animals and thought to be caused by the use of slaughter-house waste as animal feed. A similar infectious agent causes Kreutzfeld-Jacob disease in humans.

carbon footprint   measure of the impact that human activities have on the environment in terms of the amount of greenhouse gases produced. It is measured in units of carbon dioxide.

coagulate   irreversible process in which proteins 'set' when heat is applied; for example, an egg changes from a liquid to a solid during frying and cannot be changed back

cross-contamination   transfer of bacteria from a contaminated source to an uncontaminated food

culture   bacteria grown in artificial conditions

curds   protein formed when milk is treated with rennet, a starter culture, during the production of cheese

diacetyl   present in butter as a flavour and aroma agent. A synthetic version may be added to margarines.

enzymes   proteins that speed up metabolic reactions

functional foods   foods that contain an ingredient that has health-promoting properties

fungi   micro-organisms that may or may not be visible to the naked eye. There are two types: moulds and yeasts.

homogenize   process in which milk is forced through tiny holes under pressure causing the fat globules to break up and remain evenly suspended throughout. The cream does not float to the top of homogenized milk.

host   organism on which another lives as a parasite

infestation   problem caused by a large number of living things such as insects

low biological value protein   protein that does not provide all essential amino acids in sufficient quantity or type necessary for human nutrition

micro-organisms organism so small that it can only be seen with a microscope. Fungi and bacteria are micro-organisms.

modified atmosphere packaging (MAP) packaging technology in which the atmosphere inside a container is altered to extend the shelf-life of the product but retain all the food's natural characteristics (such as its colour)

mould type of fungi (micro-organism) that is multi-cellular

non-starch polysaccharide (NSP) complex carbohydrates found in foods other than starches; also called fibre or dietary fibre. NSPs may be divided into insoluble (found in wheat, maize, rice) and soluble (found in oats, beans, rye) types.

novel proteins protein foods that have been developed from new sources. For example, micro-organisms, fungi and algae have all been used to produce vegetarian protein.

organic substances of animal or plant origin; chemically their molecules contain carbon

ovo-lacto vegetarian people who will not eat meat, fish or poultry and avoid any ingredients derived from these sources (such as gelatine), but will eat eggs and dairy products

parasite animal or plant living on or in another animal or plant

pasteurized heat treatment of products such as milk; high temperature, short time (HTST) methods are often used; destroys many pathogenic micro-organisms

pathogenic causing disease, for example a pathogenic bacteria can cause food poisoning

pH method of measuring the amount of acidity or alkalinity on a logarithmic scale. The scale runs from 0 (strongly acidic) to 14 (strongly alkaline); 7 is neutral and is the pH of water.

proactive taking the initiative and attempting to change things

pulses dried peas, beans and lentils; high in protein and often used in vegetarian dishes

refrigerant substance used to make something very cold, for example the fluid that keeps a refrigerator cold

smart foods foods that have been developed through the invention of new or improved processes

spores reproductive cells of fungi; when referring to bacteria, they are produced by some bacteria when the bacteria is unable to multiply

starter culture culture of bacteria used to start the production or fermentation of a food product such as cheese

substrate substance that allows something to happen; for example, the discoloration of fruit may be caused by enzymes acting with phenolic compounds (the substrate)

vegans very strict vegetarians who will not eat any animal product or food derived from animal sources and exclude foods and products that involve the use of or the harming of animals

whey liquid that is left when curds are produced and removed during the production of cheese

yeast unicellular organism, grouped with fungi; grows on plant foods

Index